let's travel in
ENGLAND

Edited by Darlene Geis

A TRAVEL PRESS BOOK

PICTURE ACKNOWLEDGMENTS
Twenty of the photographs in this book were taken in England by Ace Williams. Full color picture 1 is from the British Travel & Holiday Association, London. Pictures 6, 8, 16 and 32 are by George Pickow from Three Lions, Inc. Pictures 11, 12, 13, 18, 21 and 24 are from Photo Researchers, Inc. Picture 27 is from Wedgwood, Ltd. For the black-and-white photographs we wish to thank the British Travel Association; British Information Services; the Bettmann Archives; J. Allan Cash from Rapho-Guillumette; Photo Researchers, Inc.; Henri Cartier-Bresson and Cornell Capa from Magnum; Lida Moser, Fritz Henle and B. Silberstein from Monkmeyer; and Ace Williams. The map was made by Enrico Arno. Designed by Mann Associates.

CONTENTS

IRELAND

SCOTLA

LONDON

Regents Park

9

Baker St.

Euston Road

Portland Pl.

Regent St.

Oxford Street

Hyde Park

Serpentine

Piccadilly

7

The Mall

32

Whitehall

8

5

Westminster Bridge

6

3

Strand

Fleet St.

Thames River

Waterloo Road

Blackfriars Road

City Rd.

1

2

to Greenwich

4

IRISH SEA

29

Hawkshea
lake
Winder m

Liverpoo

WALES

18

Severn R.

Bath

Stoneheng

23

Clovelly

21

Plymouth

ATLANTIC OCEAN

22

Land's End

ENGLISH

Locales of thirty-two full-color pictures

ENGLAND:
"THIS PRECIOUS STONE SET IN THE SILVER SEA"

WHOEVER travels through England for the first time feels some familiarity with the country. Through the eyes of her great writers people of all lands have come to know England intimately. No American can visit England without a thrill of rediscovery. The London Bridge that was falling down in a childhood nursery rhyme; Plymouth, the port from which the Mayflower sailed and whose name the Pilgrim fathers gave to the Massachusetts rock on which they first landed; Canterbury Cathedral on an April day, looking much the same as when Chaucer wrote about it five hundred years ago—these places are old friends.

Only one thing might surprise the first-time visitor to England—the small size of this great country. For England itself, exclusive of Wales and Scotland, is only 50,870 square miles—not much larger than the state of New York. The island of Great Britain sits above the English Channel to the north of France, somewhat like a lion resting on its haunches and facing westward toward Ireland and the New World. Cover the lion's head—Scotland—and its forepaws—Wales—and the broad-based triangle that remains is England. Within the small compass of this fair land a magnificent pageant of history has been played for the past two thousand years.

The coasts of England, indented in thousands of coves and harbors, are washed by the Irish Sea to the west, the North Sea to the east, and the English Channel to the south. Over these waters sailed bold adventurers—Saxons and Scandinavians from the east, and Romans and Normans from the south—whose intermingling resulted in the people, the language and the character that we know today as English. Only at the extreme southwest of the island, where Land's End thrusts out into the broad Atlantic, does England touch the open ocean upon which her destiny was shaped. No place in this island nation is more than 75 miles from the sea, and as a consequence the English became such skilled mariners that they could proudly boast, "Britannia rules the waves!"

A CLIMATE FOR HEROES

The surrounding seas have, as Shakespeare pointed out in *Richard II*, served as a defensive moat "against the envy of less happier lands." They have also, and perhaps more successfully, guarded England from the assaults of extreme heat or cold. For, thanks to the Gulf Stream, the country enjoys a moderate climate in which her people have been able to thrive and grow great.

Long before the Christian era, Britain was a fertile island, thickly forested, with marshy lowlands and green plains invitingly spread out along the coastlines facing the Continent. Only in the north and west did the land rise into the formidable mountain crags of Wales, Scotland and northwest England. Those natural divides stopped the numerous invaders who overran the lower, more level land, and that is why we find today that Scotland and Wales reflect the older Celtic civilization, while the rest of Britain has been colored by Roman, Saxon, Scandinavian and Norman influences. We see the difference in place names, and

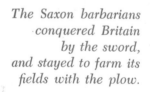

The Saxon barbarians conquered Britain by the sword, and stayed to farm its fields with the plow.

we can hear it most dramatically in the dialects of the different regions.

England's history was shaped by her geography. As we travel through the country—so small, yet so remarkably varied—we will see how each section was cast in its historic role by its geographic characteristics. The star of this fabulous pageant is London, the great capital on the Thames (TEHMZ), and we must go back two thousand years to discover its mist-shrouded beginnings.

"LONDON IS A MAN'S TOWN, THERE'S POWER IN THE AIR"

When Julius Caesar invaded Britain in 55 B.C., London was just a small Celtic hamlet on the marshy bank of the Thames. There were other towns in Britain far more important than this one that the Romans called Londinium. But under later Roman rule the site of London proved to be ideal for a bridgehead because the river narrowed there. The fabled Roman roads that ran from the Channel ports northward and westward led to this bridge, then crossed the Thames and radiated outward to crisscross the island. Around busy London Bridge the town grew and prospered, especially since the Romans engaged in active trade with the Continent.

Although the city went into eclipse during the dark years of barbarian invasions after the Romans left, by the eleventh century London was once again a wealthy commercial center. When the Anglo-Saxon king, Edward the Confessor, died, he was buried in the Abbey he had built outside the city walls at Westminster. In 1066 William the Conqueror had the crown of England placed on his Norman head in that same Abbey. For nine hundred years the majestic coronations of the English kings and queens have taken place at Westminster Abbey, which now lies well within the limits of sprawling London.

Today, Greater London encompasses 692 square miles. At its heart is the ancient City of London, that mile-square section on the north bank of the Thames which was originally contained within the Roman walls. London's history is written in the very stones of the city, as we shall see. Roman Londinium's mosaic pavements come to light in occasional excavations. The Norman Conqueror's massive stronghold, now part of the Tower of London, still stands guard at the city's water gate. And medieval Westminster Hall and the newer Houses of Parliament tell the noble story of English justice, law and government through the centuries. From Buckingham Palace the monarch's standard flies, uniting nearly a quarter of the world in allegiance to the British Crown. Modern London hums with the vitality of a great capital, and its citizens still have influence and power far beyond the confines of the city.

THE SOUTH COAST, GATEWAY
TO THE CONTINENT

Lying to the south of London are the fruitful and flowering counties of Kent, Surrey, Sussex and Hampshire. Here in the pre-Roman days were fine pastures, fields of grain, wild woods filled with game, iron mines and the little Channel ports that made this tempting land so easy of access. The Celts crossed the Channel and settled in this region. Caesar entered Britain through Dover, William the Conqueror through Hastings; St. Augustine came from Rome and founded English Christianity at Canterbury. It was across this threshold of gleaming chalk cliffs that the culture of the Mediterranean world was carried inland to the savage northerners who inhabited the island.

The South Coast is rich in history. And while history takes you by one hand, literature leads you by the other. Charles Dickens, Jane Austen, Isaak Walton, Lewis Carroll, Rudyard Kipling, Lord Tennyson all lived and wrote within this region. Mementos of their lives still remain, including the sundial in Kipling's garden in Sussex upon which he carved, as he put it, "something dreadful": IT IS LATER THAN YOU THINK.

The sharply tapered peninsula that juts westward into the Atlantic between the English Channel and the Bristol Channel has a climate warmed and tempered by the Gulf Stream. Here on the mild plains prehistoric man left his earliest traces in England. And here, in modern times, the coasts are fringed with sunny seaside resorts that make this region an unusual northern Riviera.

THE MIDLANDS, GREEN HEART OF ENGLAND

Concentrated within the small central portion of the country is much of England's beauty and her wealth, both cultural and industrial. This is the land of meandering rivers and pleasant valleys, of the Cotswold Hills and their villages of rough-stone houses. The rolling pastures were ideal for sheep and cattle, and at one time England was primarily a pastoral country. But here in the Midlands and farther north we also find England's industrial might, the iron muscle under the gentle green land. The hideous factory towns of the nineteenth century spread darkly above those places where coal was found, just as the pottery towns of Staffordshire sprang up along the line of certain valuable clay deposits. Because of the industrial revolution, a predominantly rural population was pulled off the land and jammed into crowded, ill-planned cities.

England's glory, as well as her power, is to be found in the Midlands. The silvery spires of Oxford mark one of the oldest and most venerated universities in the world. And at Stratford, on the river Avon, the most gifted writer in the English language was born. Shakespeare's birthplace has become a shrine, and his plays are performed there every summer.

East of the Midlands, the rounded bulge called East Anglia is a flat, water-laced country separated by the North Sea from the Lowlands of Europe. With its dikes, canals, windmills and tulip fields, this picturesque corner of England might be a bit of Holland moved to the opposite side of the sea. In early times these unprotected lowlands were easily raided by the seafaring Scandinavian and Saxon adventurers, who swarmed inland and eventually made this fertile land their home.

THE NORTH OF ENGLAND, PRODUCTIVE POWER

North of the Midlands the land takes on a different character. Here are the windswept moorlands of Yorkshire where the Brontë sisters wrote their tempestuous tales—among them *Jane Eyre* and *Wuthering Heights*. Here, too, is the scenic grandeur of the Lake District with its mountains, wooded valleys and still blue lakes that inspired the poetry of Wordsworth, Coleridge and Southey. In Northumberland, near the Scottish border, the old Roman Wall of Hadrian, grass-grown and deserted now, winds over the desolate moors.

The people of the North are energetic and forceful. They are the hard-working businessmen and manufacturers of England. The leisurely Southerners, who are more reserved, speak—in the upper classes—with the accents of Oxford and Cambridge, and center their interest on London and the government. The South governs, while the North produces.

Emperor Hadrian built this Roman wall to mark the northern boundary of Britain.

TIGHT LITTLE ISLAND

From the gleaming white cliffs of Dover to the brooding and romantic Border Country, from the farthest tip of Land's End to the marshes of East Anglia, you cannot travel more than 400 miles across England's length or breadth. Yet, more than 42,000,000 people are crammed into this little space, a condition that surely has had some effect upon the national character. English reserve and the cherishing of privacy and individual rights are probably the outcome of having to live crowded so closely together.

But if the English are crowded on their home island they have compensated for it by fanning out over the globe into the empire upon which the sun never sets. Now the empire has become a vast commonwealth of nations scattered over the wide world but loosely held together in their allegiance to the British Crown. England has come through twenty centuries of history, absorbing her conquerors, adapting to the changing times, and yet maintaining her own colorful and individual character. As we travel through the country we will see this indomitable Englishness in every shire and hamlet, as well as on the busy streets of London.

Piccadilly Circus at night is London's liveliest square.

let's travel in

ENGLAND

TOWER WARDER:
GUARDIAN
OF THE PAST

DRESSED in the scarlet, black and gold uniform of the Tower Warders, this man symbolizes the stalwart English spirit. He and the Tower that he guards are a fitting introduction to a country whose colorful history is woven into its present life. Nine hundred years ago William the Conqueror built his White Tower on the bank of the Thames below London to show the English that they were from then on a subject people. But little by little, over the years, the Normans from across the Channel were absorbed by the English whom they ruled. And William's original Tower of London is now only the core of a much vaster fortification built by later English kings and still used today.

A gloomy procession of famous men and women has passed behind these grim walls. Two unfortunate wives of Henry VIII, Anne Boleyn and Catherine Howard, were executed here. Elizabeth I was confined briefly in the Tower before she became queen, but it was her happy fate to mount the throne instead of the scaffold. And as recently as World War II the Tower served as a prison for spies.

The Tower Warders still wear the costume designed for them in Tudor times, but they are all retired Army men with fine war records, and their modern medals and ribbons make a brave show on the old Tudor scarlet. They are frequently confused with the Yeomen of the Guard, the monarch's special guards who wear nearly the same uniform and are called "Beefeaters." In this picture the Chief Warder is carrying his badge of office, a staff topped by a silver model of the White Tower. It is his duty to lock up at night, and he and the other Warders leave the Tower only on state occasions when they must take the Crown Jewels to the monarch. On these traditional missions they travel by twentieth-century automobile.

16

TOWER BRIDGE: LONDON'S WATER GATE

SPANNING the Thames just below the gray stone battlements of the Tower is this river gateway to London, Tower Bridge. Down river lies the East End and the Port of London, crowded with ships from all over the world. Up river, the Thames winds through the heart of London, a blue-gray thoroughfare that has brought power and riches to the city on its banks.

Until 1739 there was only one bridge over the Thames, the famous London Bridge. It was made of stone and had been completed at the beginning of the thirteenth century on the site of earlier wooden spans. Wooden houses, shops and a chapel sprang up along the length of London Bridge, and at its two ends stood hideous spiked gates where the heads of traitors were impaled. Traffic was heavy on the crowded old bridge, but the river currents were treacherous for boatmen. And so the saying was born: "London Bridge was made for wise men to go over and for fools to go under."

London's East End is the home of the Pearlies—Cockney peddlers who sport these pearl-trimmed clothes.

The picturesque old bridge, where Shakespeare undoubtedly browsed at the bookshops, and where the artists Hogarth and Holbein once lived, was torn down in 1832 after the new London Bridge was completed. Tower Bridge was created some sixty years later just below London Bridge. Both bridge and fortress seem to guard the cultivated life of the city from the intrusions of foreign ships, come to do business in the Port.

18

VICTORIA EMBANKMENT: CRUISING ON THE THAMES

THE Thames is London and London is the Thames," is an adage that applies to this modern city as truly as it did to Roman Londinium. The river has always been the city's Main Street, linking its commerce with the sea and the distant lands beyond the sea. Until the nineteenth century, London's streets were narrow muddy lanes, and it was safer and pleasanter for her citizens to travel by water whenever possible. English kings have boated on the Thames in barges decked with flowers, while servants sprayed perfume into the air and musicians played sweet serenades. And though today it is not necessary to use the river in preference to the streets, boat cruises are still a popular form of transportation.

In this picture you can see several of the river boats at their dock below the Victoria Embankment near Westminster Bridge. They are not decked with flowers, and no one sprays perfume or fills the air with music, but for a few shillings you can sail the Thames almost as grandly as a king of old. And you will have a guide with a megaphone to point out the sights.

Directly above the Embankment are the striped brick buildings of New Scotland Yard, known to every reader of mystery stories as the headquarters of the Metropolitan Police. "New" Scotland Yard is some seventy years old, but when the police moved to these buildings from their old quarters, the name came with them. Their old offices were located at Great Scotland Yard where the Scottish kings and their ambassadors had their London residence several centuries ago. History in this city never dies—it simply stays alive in some modern incarnation. When you board a motor launch here you can travel up to Kew Gardens, Richmond and Hampton Court. Or you can sail downstream beyond the Tower to the Port of London, or farther still to Greenwich on the outskirts of London. The river carries you timelessly past the living landmarks of history.

CLOCK
AT GREENWICH:
UNIVERSAL
TIMEPIECE

IN GREENWICH, time is of the essence. This section of London, which was once a separate village, is the geographic starting point of the earth's longitude. The zero meridian, from which the east-west measurements of the globe, and time, are reckoned, runs through the old Royal Observatory. On top of the east turret of the Observatory is a mast crowned by the famous red time-ball. At exactly 1 P.M. each day the ball drops, indicating precise Greenwich Mean Time. All the world sets its clocks by the time computed here—which is known more poetically as Universal Time.

The Royal Observatory was founded in Greenwich in 1675. The vigorous Englishmen whose ships were supreme on the seven seas were also conquering the heavens and earth by measurements and astronomical observations. In 1946 the Astronomer Royal and his colleagues packed up their telescopes and moved the Observatory down to Sussex, where the clearer air was better for their observations. They had to leave the zero meridian where it was, so Greenwich continues to be the arbiter of time. In this picture we see what must certainly be the most authoritative clock in the world. It is connected with the actual mechanism that determines the time, and is set into a wall of the old Observatory. Below it are the official British measurements for a yard, two feet, a foot, six inches. Years ago, when there were no standard rulers available, people could come here and check the correct measurements—straight from the royal yardstick.

Greenwich is full of reminders of England's seafaring greatness. The National Maritime Museum traces the history of England's long and dramatic conquest of the sea. And the Royal Naval College, where tomorrow's admirals are being trained, used to be a home for retired sea dogs who had fought in England's great naval battles. Time—past, present and future—is represented here.

BIG BEN: THE VOICE OF LONDON

WE HAVE taken the motor launch back to Westminster Bridge. Here facing us is a corner of the Houses of Parliament with the familiar Clock Tower. The great bell which booms the hours high over London is a thirteen-and-a-half-ton behemoth known affectionately as Big Ben. When it was hung in the last century, Sir Benjamin Hall was Chief Commissioner of Works, and his name is now immortalized in this bronze bell. Big Ben has been heard in the farthest corners of the civilized world, thanks to the carrying power of radio. And the influence of the "Mother of Parliaments," above which the great clock rises, has been just as far-reaching.

Ever since 1215, when a group of barons forced King John to sign the Magna Charta, or "Great Charter," law has been supreme in England, and even kings have bowed to it. Laws are made in the imposing Gothic pile where the House of Lords and the House of Commons meet. Although the building dates only from the middle of the last century, actually Parliament has always had its home on this site, in the old Palace of Westminster.

For many years there had been talk of building a new Parliament House, and in 1834 David Hume rose in Commons and made an impassioned but unsuccessful plea for a larger House. Some months later fire swept through the old buildings and all but the venerable Westminster Hall and part of St. Stephen's Chapel were destroyed. At which a wag commented, "There is Mr. Hume's motion, carried without an amendment!"

Sprawling over eight acres, this vast complex of buildings and courts is like a giant maze out of which, miraculously, the clear and logical British laws emerge. Big Ben has sounded the hours while men like Disraeli, Gladstone, Lloyd George and Churchill made history in the Parliament below.

WESTMINSTER ABBEY: BRITISH PANTHEON

BEHIND the Houses of Parliament stands England's national shrine, Westminster Abbey. Its origin dates back to the legendary days of Saxon London when a group of Benedictine monks founded a church on the banks of the Thames beyond the city walls. It became known as "West Minster," or the monastery to the west. In the eleventh century, Edward the Confessor rebuilt the Abbey on a more magnificent scale, and when he was canonized his tomb became one of the most revered miracle-working shrines in England.

Today, when we stand beneath the lofty vaulted roof of the Abbey, we are surrounded by the tombs and monuments of England's great. The rulers—Plantagenet, Tudor, Stuart and Hanoverian—are ranged round the shrine of the Confessor like stately planets circling a sun. The lesser stars of England's history—her statesmen, writers, artists, musicians, inventors and worthy citizens of times long past—have their tombs or monuments scattered throughout the nave and transept of the church.

The vaulted passage of Burlington Arcade lends stateliness to a street of shops.

Walking through the Abbey, with its ancient stone glowing in a golden light, you feel yourself in the presence of the national genius. The coronation of a British monarch in this church takes on an added luster and significance.

TRAFALGAR SQUARE: OASIS IN THE CITY

LONDONERS are as passionately devoted to the beauties and charms of the countryside as are their fellow Englishmen. So they have imbedded bits and pieces of rural England in their metropolis. Stone buildings are decorated with flower boxes sprouting greenery and bright blossoms. Blocks of gray masonry give way to refreshing squares, where grass and trees grow and bird songs mingle with traffic noises. And the parks, which William Pitt the Elder called "the lungs of London," are more like country meadows transplanted to the heart of the city.

One of the best-loved squares in London is Trafalgar Square, which memorializes Lord Nelson's greatest sea victory. Towering above the square on a tall column, a heroic Nelson stands, and around the column's base four bronze lions take their ease, symbols of empire. In place of the bounding main, the fountains we see here send their jets high in the air where, to an imaginative eye, they resemble the blown spray of a rough sea.

On a fine summer's day the square is crowded with people who manage to escape for a while from the urban confines of London and enjoy the open sky and splashing water in the tree-fringed square. Starlings and pigeons have made Trafalgar Square their sanctuary, and in the early evening, when the fountains are turned off, their cooing and chattering bring the sounds of nature to city ears.

Trafalgar Square is in the West End of London—the fashionable section of the city where luxury shops, theaters, fine restaurants, and distinguished mansions and hotels create a separate little world of privilege. Piccadilly, Bond Street, Regent Street, Berkeley (BARK-*lee*) and Grosvenor (GROVE-*ner*) Squares, Mayfair and St. James are West End names familiar to many people. The West End wears its affluence comfortably—it has had it for three hundred years.

29

BUCKINGHAM
PALACE:
HORSE GUARDS
ON PARADE

MORNINGS in London begin with scarlet-coated pageantry, whether the sun shines, as it does in this picture, or a yellow fog mutes the bright colors. The Horse Guards, also known as the Household Cavalry, are splendid in their plumed helmets as they ride up the Mall with a brave jingling of spurs. Behind them we can see the gray mass of Buckingham Palace. At the palace each morning, there is another ceremony when the Guard changes to the strains of martial music, while an admiring crowd watches the best free show in London. It is a stirring sight to foreigners and British alike, and a daily reminder to all of the firm vow that "Britons never will be slaves."

Buckingham Palace is the Queen's London residence, but St. James Palace is still the official Court of England. (That is why we speak of an Ambassador to Britain as being accredited to "The Court of St.

This tall Guardsman is unflinchingly dignified, in spite of the mischievous Boy Scouts below.

James.") In the eighteenth century the Duke of Buckingham built a country house on the site of the present palace. Buckingham House underwent numerous alterations that changed it from a country place to its present palatial form. It was Queen Victoria who chose this relatively unhistoric and unpretentious building for her home. The Royal Family has lived there ever since, at the heart of the British capital. And in times of rejoicing or crisis Englishmen rally to the gates of Buckingham Palace in a spontaneous demonstration of devotion.

MADAME TUSSAUD'S: HISTORY IN WAX

THERE is more than enough living history in the very streets of London, but Englishmen seem to have an insatiable curiosity about the past, and at Madame Tussaud's famous waxworks they can satisfy it. Collected in this museum are kings, queens, presidents, tyrants, movie stars and a Chamber of Horrors peopled with blood-curdling murderers.

Madame Tussaud was a remarkable woman who spent nine years of her youth in Versailles (*vair*-SIGH), during the reign of Louis XVI, teaching the French courtiers to model in wax. During the Revolution and the Reign of Terror that followed it, her skilled hands were kept busy at the gruesome task of making wax masks of the victims of the guillotine. When she moved to England with her gallery of wax portraits, it was an immediate success, and the present Tussaud who runs it is the great-great-grandson of the adventurous founder.

So realistic are these figures that, whenever possible, their clothing is authentic. The elaborate costumes are complete even to undergarments, which are changed once a week. Each morning the wax people are freshly groomed—their clothes are brushed and arranged neatly, hair and beards are combed, shoes and buttons polished. The illustrious personages, even in effigy, face the world at their best.

In this picture Madame Tussaud has taken us back to the eleventh century. But this is no ordinary scene of medieval domesticity. The lady is embroidering nothing less than the fabulous Bayeux (*bay*-YOU) tapestry, that carefully worked strip of cloth which is a picture-story of the Norman Conquest. No one knows who really made it, but tradition assigns it to Matilda, wife of William the Conqueror. Perhaps that is William standing at his lady's shoulder and saying, "No, no, Matilda, that's not *quite* the way it happened. You women don't really understand about war."

WINDSOR CASTLE: FABLED BATTLEMENTS

ABOUT twenty-two miles west of London, where the Thames curves lazily between emerald lawns, William the Conqueror built a mighty stronghold on a chalk cliff that rises steeply above the countryside. From this vantage point William could dominate the Midlands as well as the approach to London. For nearly nine hundred years, English sovereigns have made Windsor their home and behind these gray stone walls some of the most colorful scenes in history have been played. It was to Windsor Castle that Henry V, the victor of Agincourt, brought his French bride Catherine, and here their son was born. Henry VI became king at the age of nine months when his father met an untimely death in France. Across the river from Windsor lies Eton College, established by Henry VI in 1440, one of the few accomplishments of his miserable reign.

At Windsor the Most Noble Order of the Garter was founded some six hundred years ago. The popular story has it that at a ball in the Round Tower the Countess of Salisbury lost her garter while dancing with the King. To silence his snickering courtiers, Edward III chivalrously picked up the garter and placed it below his own knee. Then he pronounced the French words that have been the motto of the Order of the Garter ever since: "Honi soit qui mal y pense" (*oh-nee* SWAH *kee mahl ee* PAHNSS)—"Evil to him who evil thinks." There are only thirty-five members of this noble order at present, and one of them is the Honorable Winston Churchill. The letters "K.G." after an Englishman's name mean that he has been made a Knight of the Garter by his sovereign.

St. George's Chapel at Windsor, one of the finest Gothic chapels in England, is the imposing scene of the ceremonies of the Order of the Garter. But in our time Windsor Castle is best remembered as the place from which a sad-voiced King Edward VIII announced his abdication and gave up his crown for "the woman I love."

34

ETON SCHOOLBOYS: A GREAT TRADITION

FOR more than five hundred years the mellow brick buildings of Eton College have housed the students of one of England's greatest schools. Over the centuries Eton has acquired traditions that create a special world and way of life for Etonians. The broad white collars and black tail-coats worn by these boys identify them immediately as students of Eton, as do the shiny black top hats worn now only on special occasions. Students below a certain height have to wear the short, collarless Eton jacket. One of the hallowed traditions of the school occurs each year on the birthday of Henry VI, the founder of Eton. A group of students makes the trip to the Tower of London and there the solemn schoolboys place a red rose on the very spot where the king died.

Eton, Harrow and Winchester are called "public schools," but actually they are private to the point of being exclusive. The cream of England's upper-class young men get the equivalent of their high school education at these venerable institutions, and many of them grow up to become the nation's leaders. Eton builds character as well as minds, and the boys are subjected to a rigorous training in which sports and sportsmanship figure importantly. The Duke of Wellington was not exaggerating when he made his famous statement: "The battle of Waterloo was won on the playing fields of Eton."

Students at Cambridge University wear straw boaters and blazers for their May Week festivities.

CRICKET MATCH: NATIONAL GAME

THE bright green English lawns are particularly suited to the national game. On a summer's afternoon, when white-clad figures move across the turf in the dignified patterns of a cricket match, even spectators who do not understand the game find it beautiful to watch. Cricket was originally played on village greens, as we see it here, and on the playing fields of a few schools. Now the most important matches each season take place in London at Lord's.

The audience for the annual Eton-Harrow match at Lord's is elegant. The men wear top hats and cutaways, the women float by in pretty garden-party dresses. Their garb is a good indication of how highly the English esteem sports. All the virtues of the national character are dramatized on the playing field—honor, team spirit, fair play, the desire to win and the ability to lose with grace and courage. Spectators and athletes alike dress up as a salute to chivalry, whether it is for a boat race at Henley, a horse race at Ascot, or cricket at Lord's.

Little by little this gentlemen's game has become more democratic. There are now professional cricketers who are called "Players," while the amateurs are still known as "Gentlemen." Both may play on the same team, but until recently each group had a separate dressing room. The rules of cricket have changed very little in the more than two hundred years of the game's history. The batsman stands in front of the wicket, while the bowler hurls the ball at him overhand. The batsman must try to hit any ball that might otherwise strike against the wicket and put him out. There are only two innings in the game, and a first-class cricket match lasts three days, from noon to six o'clock. It is a leisurely game, played under English skies on long summer afternoons, and watched with the restrained enthusiasm that is a hallmark of the British gentry.

NORFOLK BROADS: SMOOTH-WATER SAILING

SPORTS-MINDED Englishmen are keen on games like cricket, soccer and Rugby, but there are other sporting pursuits to which they devote much of their leisure, too. Hunting with hounds, shooting, fishing in the quiet trout streams, bird-watching, hiking, and almost any outdoor activity that involves a picnic lunch are favorite English pastimes. But for these island people, descendants of bold seafarers, boating is the most enjoyable recreation of all.

The rivers that wind through green fields and shady woods are ideal for those who favor rowing. But here, where eastern England curves out into the North Sea, is the vacation land for devotees of smooth-water sailing. The Norfolk Broads is a low, flat expanse of coastal land where sluggish streams widen into shallow lagoons. Along their shores charming villages, inns, and the ruins of old abbeys and castles give the sailor a fascinating change of scene as his boat glides along.

The chain of rivers and lagoons provides about two hundred miles of navigable water. Sailboats and motor cruisers can be rented by the week, and each boat has a small dinghy attached, for exploring the shallow little byways that branch off delightfully to secret spots. A good companion, a picnic hamper, cloudless sky and smooth sailing, then a friendly inn to come home to—this is English vacationing at its best.

Old salts gather at the waterfront where tall masts sway and the air smells of the sea.

41

YE OLDE
LEATHER BOTTLE:
DICKENS'
FAVORITE INN

THROUGH the centuries, while kings and nobles enjoyed more luxurious pleasures, the ordinary folk of England had their plainer delights. The little inns that served tankards of nut-brown ale and the simple but hearty food of the country were the backbone of merry England. Robin Hood and his men played pranks at the Blue Boar; Samuel Johnson, Boswell and Oliver Goldsmith talked the night away at the Cheshire Cheese; and Charles Dickens' Pickwick Clubmen met at the Leather Bottle, which we see here. Some English literary characters are as real as their creators, and when we stand before the Leather Bottle in Cobham, Pickwick and his friends seem more than ever to have been real people.

The Leather Bottle was old when Dickens wrote about it, having been built in 1629. Englishmen through all the ages must have loved their taverns—they have taken such good care of them. Looking up at the second floor windows, slightly askew with age now, we realize that one of them was the very lattice window thrown open by Pickwick the night he stayed at the inn. Dickens' description of the "parlour" tallies exactly with the old room now. And when we step into this clean and commodious village ale-house, we can almost hear jolly, bald Mr. Pickwick proposing, "Let us celebrate this happy meeting with a convivial glass."

An English pub is a homey place for a neighborly glass and a game of darts.

DOVER BEACH: BENEATH THE WHITE CLIFFS

DOVER looks peaceful and gay in this picture. The bright colors of bathing suits and towels make a confetti pattern on the resort beach that has been an important landing place since pre-Roman times. The Strait of Dover separating England from France is a mere twenty miles wide here, and has even been crossed by swimmers—in 1926 Gertrude Ederle swam it in about fourteen hours.

The famed white cliffs rise behind the narrow beach and are broken by a river valley where the town of Dover has grown up. On the heights above, an ancient fortress guards the approach to the "Saxon Shore." Its grim, gray castle has been known for centuries as the Key to England. Near the castle stand the ruins of the oldest building in England —a Roman lighthouse built about 50 A.D.

These buildings have been witness to a long march of events. Watling Street, the Roman road from the Channel to London, starts here and at one time the Roman legions passed this way. Richard the Lionhearted and his knights assembled on this beach before the third Crusade, and Charles II landed at Dover when he returned from his French exile. The flawless sky above the castle and lighthouse was one of the terrible aerial battlefields during World War II, but little of this is remembered by the bathers on Dover beach today.

The brilliant white chalk cliffs gave England its early name of Albion.

45

H.M.S. VICTORY: NELSON'S HONORED FLAGSHIP

AT A dock in Portsmouth, the *Victory* rests at her final moorings. This brightly painted man-of-war once flew Lord Nelson's ensign from her mast and carried him to his devastating triumph over Napoleon's navy. The great sea battle took place off Cape Trafalgar near the Strait of Gibraltar in 1805. Nelson lost his life, but England gained absolute supremacy of the seas, and the *Victory* in Portsmouth's dockyard is now a place of national pilgrimage.

These beautiful but deadly line-of-battle ships were the small island's chief strength when she stood alone against Napoleon's Europe. The black and yellow hulls under towering white sails must have been an awesome sight in their day. The *Victory*, lying quietly at anchor now, her tall masts bare, still strikes awe into the hearts of her visitors.

You cannot step aboard this gallant ship without marveling at the spirit of the sailors who manned her—from the lowliest cabin boy to the great Admiral himself. In her day the *Victory* had a crew of eight hundred men. They lived, often for years at a time, crowded into the two lower gun decks, with their hammocks slung above the cannon they tended. The decks were only 186 feet long, and the ship weighed a little more than 2,000 tons, close quarters in the best of circumstances. Imagine it under battle conditions, choked with the smoke and stench of the muzzle-loaders that bristled from these airless decks! At Trafalgar the *Victory*'s wheel was shot away by a French broadside, and men were hitched to tackles that pulled a giant tiller, maneuvering the ship by dint of sheer muscle power.

Nelson was picked off by an enemy sniper as he walked the quarter-deck during the blazing height of the battle. The frail little Admiral was carried down to the lowest of the five decks where a ship's surgeon worked by candlelight. It was here that Nelson, dying, uttered his deathless words, "Thank God, I have done my duty."

46

RIVER AT WINCHESTER: THE COMPLEAT ANGLER

THE English have cultivated the arts of peace no less than the arts of war. Their pleasant land, which they have had to fight to preserve, has been a source of enjoyment and inspiration in the golden years between wars. In this picture we are in a quiet garden behind the old mill at Winchester. Three hundred years ago Izaak Walton fished this very trout stream, the River Itchen, and wrote about it in *The Compleat Angler:*

> *"I in these flowery meads would be;*
> *These crystal springs should solace me,*
> *To whose harmonious bubbling noise,*
> *I with my angle would rejoice."*

A great deal of water has flowed under this mill since Winchester's earliest days. Britons, Romans, Saxons and Normans lived, each in their turn, in this city on the River Itchen. Winchester was the capital of the old Saxon kingdom of Wessex, and in 827 Egbert of Wessex was crowned here, the first king of all the English. Alfred the Great organized his campaign against the Danes from Winchester, and he made his city a great center of learning. England's oldest "public" school, Winchester College, was founded here in 1382, and on one of its walls is a Latin inscription that means "Learn, leave or be licked," a no-nonsense attitude toward education that has made English schools among the finest in the world.

Through the eventful centuries the River Itchen has gone its peaceful way, temptingly stocked with trout. Perhaps it offered kings and scholars a chance to escape from their heavier duties. Certainly men long before and after Izaak Walton have been delighted to say, as he did, "I have laid aside business, and gone a-fishing."

COUNTRY INN:
ENGLISH
HOSPITALITY

THE pleasant countryside of England is dotted with inns, most of them hundreds of years old. Great lumbering stagecoaches used to travel along the winding roads, and the cobbled courtyard of an inn marked the end of each day's journey. Travelers could always count on a hearty meal, a warm fire and a place to sleep after hours of jolting along rough roads.

Today, sleek little English sports cars hum through the quiet countryside, and their destination is frequently one of the charming old inns just because the food served there is superlative. England does not have a reputation for gastronomy, yet its regional dishes, found in these country inns, can measure up to the best in the world.

In this picture we see the courtyard of the New Inn (five hundred years new) in Gloucester (GLAHS-*tur*). The waiter is serving a tray of cheeses, among them the local Double Gloucester, a mellow product made from milk and cream. Cheshire and Stilton are two other renowned English cheeses—delicious with a slice of bread and a cool drink when you stop for wayside refreshments.

But to really appreciate the food of the country you should sample the dishes of the various regions. Broiled steaks and chops are served with chips (French fried potatoes in American English). Smoked trout is a delicacy unrivaled even in France. And "soused fish" is the pungent result of cooking fish in vinegar with onions, cloves, pepper and bay leaf. Hearty steak-and-kidney pie or "jugged hare" drenched with a rich, gamy sauce are delectable examples of the food that may be served in country inns.

John Bull has always been depicted as a jolly man with a well-rounded bay window. After sampling the generous fare of his inns, we know how he got that way.

MYSTERIOUS STONEHENGE: ANCIENT MONUMENT

LONG before there was a John Bull, the early settlers of this island lived on the broad green stretch of Salisbury Plain. It is a lonely place today, with no sign of human life. The mysterious stones we are looking at in this picture are balanced in their strange designs, as if some giant child had built with crude blocks. They are all that remain of the ancient people who lived here 4,000 years ago.

Who were these primitive men and how did they manage to hoist stones that weigh fifty tons and more? What was the meaning of this huge double circle with its rough-hewn pillars and doorways? Scientists have asked these and many other puzzling questions, but so far they can only guess at the answers. Some think the ancient Druids performed their rites in this solemn circle of stone. Others believe that sun-worshippers from the Mediterranean came to this distant land when the Channel was a dry valley on the Continent, and the Thames a tributary of the Rhine. Stonehenge (which comes from the Saxon word *Stanhengist*, or "hanging stones") might also have been an enormous calendar, its changing shadows indicating to the people the cycle of the seasons and telling them when it was time to sow their crops. People and crops have vanished, but the stones stand fast, stubbornly keeping their secrets from us.

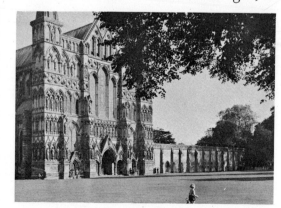

English stonemasons and sculptors reached the peak of their art in Gothic cathedrals like Salisbury.

SALISBURY CATHEDRAL: SOARING MASTERPIECE

THE crude stonework of prehistoric Stonehenge makes us marvel at primitive man. As Samuel Johnson said about women's preaching, "It is not done well; but you are suprised to find it done at all." But in Salisbury Cathedral the genius and artistry of man the builder has reached its fullest flower, and here we stand awestruck at the beauty he can create.

English cathedrals are seldom crowded in among other buildings. They stand apart in a parklike close where fine old trees shadow a velvet lawn, and the miracle of Gothic stone and glass rises from the earth like a growing thing. At Salisbury the park area is so spacious that we can stand well back and get the full impact of that slender spire—the loftiest in England—reaching upward out of the masonry. John Constable, the great English landscape painter, captured the magnificence of grass and trees and church in some of his most famous pictures.

Salisbury Cathedral is a noble example of the rekindling of English genius after the centuries of barbarian darkness. In prehistoric times the men of Stonehenge probably had a camp at Old Sarum, a hilly site about a mile and a half from Salisbury. Then much later, the Romans arrived, and their roads and villas gave the landscape a more civilized appearance. The day came when the legions were recalled to Rome and the Britons were left to face the barbarian menace on their own. Old Sarum was the last British outpost in the South to fall before the wild Saxons, and under them, all the refinements of Rome were forgotten. Not until the conquering Normans settled here hundreds of years later did buildings of stone rise again in England. Old Sarum was abandoned in favor of a fresh site on lower ground, and Salisbury Cathedral was built in the new town. Its majestic design reflects the vigor of medieval Englishmen, in whom Saxon and Norman strains united to form a bold new breed.

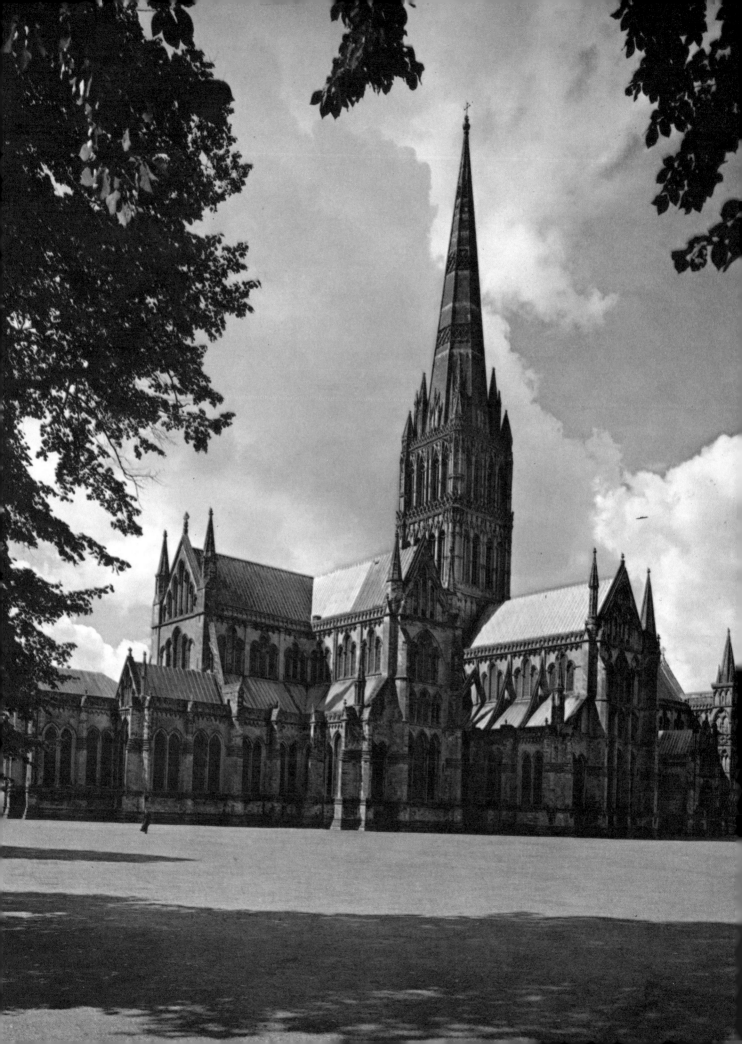

FARMER IN DEVON: PLACID COUNTRYSIDE

IN THE fertile, rolling counties of the West Country, the farmers tend their land carefully. Men like this one are the descendants of Saxon and Viking invaders, and their energy and strength and independence of spirit have become part of the national character. One British writer has said that an Englishman is "a barbarian who has been tamed by a mild climate." Certainly it is true in Devon where the bountiful earth has been conducive to a life of peaceful pleasures.

The thick clotted cream of Devonshire and its tangy apple cider are tastes that are as memorable as the countryside. As we look out over the sun-dappled landscape we appreciate how rich this earth is, how painstakingly each plot has been cultivated, and how everything here is scaled down to the small proportions of the country. Neat little fields are stitched together with tidy hedgerows; toy villages and miniature cottages nestle in the hollows. Now we can understand the Englishman's deep love of his land, expressed in Shakespeare's noble lines:

> *"This happy breed of men,*
> *this little world,*
> *This precious stone set in*
> *the silver sea . . .*
> *This blessed plot, this*
> *earth, this realm,*
> *this England."*

The towns of England have a mellow rustic beauty. This is Richmond in Yorkshire.

LAND'S END:
THE TIP
OF CORNWALL

THE long peninsula at the southwest of England narrows sharply beyond Devon and becomes the romantic and rock-cliffed duchy of Cornwall. This little point of land, whose balmy climate is a gift from the Gulf Stream, was inhabited by an ancient people. Greek traders, and possibly even the Phoenicians before them, visited this distant outpost of the known world a thousand years or more before the Christian era. Gold and pearls and precious metals were the wealth of Britain in those far-away days.

Much later, Cornwall became one of the isolated pockets of Celtic civilization, along with Ireland, Scotland and Wales. Its customs, its language, its saints and even its folk tales were distinctively its own. Many of the Celtic Britons fled across the water to what is now Brittany in France, taking their colorful civilization with them, and Brittany and Cornwall have much in common to this day.

St. Michael's Mount on the Cornish coast is almost identical with Mont-St.-Michel across the Channel.

At one time this granite headland pointing westward into an uncharted ocean was not only Land's End—it was world's end, and Cornwall was remote and strange. With the discovery of America the rocky finger took on a new significance—"Westward the course of empire takes its way." England was no longer at the edge of the known world, and her ships sailed on to brave adventures far beyond the point of Land's End.

HIGH STREET, CLOVELLY: TOURISTS' DELIGHT

SIXTY years ago Clovelly (*kloh*-VEL-*ih*) was a fishing village on the Devon coast—charming, quaint, picturesque, and doomed by these very qualities to be discovered and then overrun by tourists. But in spite of the holiday throngs and summer painters, something of Clovelly's beauty still comes through to us.

In this picture we are looking down the steep cobbled slope of High Street. The street drops in steps and stages from the cliff against which the town is built, to the little cove and stone pier below. The pier was engineered six hundred years ago and has kept Clovelly's fishing fleet in a snug harbor ever since.

In the old days a stream rushed down one side of High Street, and the houses on that side had little bridges built over the water. The brook has been diverted and it flows behind the houses now, leaving High Street free for the torrent of tourists. No cars or bicycles can run on this steep slope and the donkeys that used to be the villagers' only vehicles are weighed down by lazy visitors today.

Yet, to anyone who remembers Charles Kingsley's *Westward Ho!*, Clovelly and its neighboring "little white fishing village" of Bideford (BID-*ih-ferd*) are still recognizable. These were the coastal towns whose boys were brought up in the hardy seafaring tradition that was England's strength. The youngsters knew that there was "to landward, all richness, softness and peace; to seaward, a waste and howling wilderness of rock and roller. . . ." Kingsley's hero—and many another local boy—chose to follow the sea that lay to the west, and he sailed off to fight against the Spanish Armada. England's maritime greatness owes much to the charming fishing villages of Devon and Cornwall. Nelson's victory at Trafalgar and Drake's defeat of the Spanish Armada were made possible by the young sailors who grew up on this coast.

61

LORD MAYOR OF BATH: SPLENDID OFFICIAL

THE simple seaside villages of the southwest coast are a sharp contrast to the nearby city of Bath, at one time the most fashionable resort in England. We can see its elegance reflected in this stately room where the Lord Mayor stands, a modern man dressed in the medieval robes of his office. His fur-trimmed cloak, heavy gold chain and the two elaborate maces that are symbols of his authority are carry-overs from the days when the Lord Mayor represented the power and wealth of the citizenry. Rich merchants and influential guild members saw to it that the cities were governed by one of their own elected people rather than by a member of the nobility. Democracy came to the cities before it spread through the rest of the country.

One of the most famous Lord Mayors of London was Dick Whittington. According to legend he had been a poor orphan boy who risked his only possession—a cat—as an investment in his master's merchant ship. The ship came in with wealth for all, and Dick left his master's kitchen to become a successful merchant. Eventually, the once-shabby orphan wore the magnificent robes of the Lord Mayor of London.

The Shakespeare Memorial on the banks of the Avon is a shrine for admirers of the Bard's plays.

The Lord Mayor of Bath presides over a city that was founded by the Romans in 54 A.D. when they discovered hot springs there. The city reached the height of its prosperity as a favorite watering-place in the eighteenth century, and it owes the graceful buildings for which it is famous to that great architectural period.

STRATFORD-ON-AVON: ANNE HATHAWAY'S COTTAGE

ABOUT sixty miles north of Bath we come to the thatched roofs and half-timbered houses of Stratford. This old market town near the Cotswold Hills would probably have gone on dreaming quietly through the years if one of its local boys had not made good. Because of William Shakespeare, Stratford plays host to nearly a quarter of a million visitors each year, and has enjoyed a booming "Shakespeare Industry." Each year, during an April-to-October Festival, the Bard's plays are performed here at the Shakespeare Memorial Theater. The old buildings of the town are more romantic than the modern theater, but in Stratford, as in Denmark, Hamlet's dictum holds true, and "the play's the thing."

Sentimentalists can journey across the fields beyond the town, as we have done in this picture, to see Anne Hathaway's cottage. The Tudor farmhouse with its gentle thatched roof and country garden was the courting place of eighteen-year-old Will and his twenty-six-year-old bride. Tourists throng to its quiet garden and file through the rough-timbered rooms where Shakespeare once wooed Anne. Cameras click enthusiastically, as if the tranquil magic of this place could be carried home in a snapshot.

Shakespeare, himself, must finally have felt the peaceful attraction of his native town. At the age of twenty he had left his wife in Stratford while he went to London. There he made his fortune and lived the exciting life of an actor-writer in the fabulous hurly-burly of the Elizabethan age. But he came back to Stratford for good when he was forty-seven and famous, and he chose to finish out his days in the calm of his native town. Perhaps he was thinking of the cottage in this picture when he wrote in one of his sonnets:

"That is my home of love; if I have ranged,
Like him that travels, I return again."

65

CHIPPING CAMPDEN: COTSWOLD MARKET TOWN

THE tranquillity that we sensed even in tourist-thronged Stratford lies warm and quiet over the neighboring villages. There is a peaceful charm about this part of the country. The very names of the sleepy Cotswold towns summon up a picture of a pastoral world—Chipping Campden, Great Tew, Shipton-under-Wychwood, Cross Hands, Moreton-in-Marsh. Like Anne Hathaway's cottage, they speak of quiet times.

In the days when the wool trade flourished in England, the Cotswold Hills were fat grazing grounds for sheep. From the twelfth through the seventeenth centuries, the town we see here was an important market center (Chipping means market), and the beautiful old stone buildings were put up by medieval wool merchants. Their prosperity is reflected in the sturdy and enduring houses made of the distinctive local limestone, weathered now to a golden gray.

During the picturesque centuries of the Middle Ages, wool was regarded as "the flower and strength and revenue and blood of England." Then, toward the end of the eighteenth century, cotton became

The English country parlor is changeless— cozy and cluttered with the souvenirs of a lifetime.

the most important textile in England, and big industrial cities sprang up where coal and power were available. The old wool towns have lingered on ever since, dreamy and unhurried, as though a giant hand had stopped their clocks two hundred years ago.

66

WEDGWOOD
POTTER:
STOKE-ON-TRENT

IN THE industrial valley of the Trent River, there is a group of smoky factory towns called The Potteries. Here, the manufacture of earthenware objects—useful, if not beautiful—was a simple peasant craft until about two hundred years ago. Then Josiah Wedgwood, who was descended from a long line of potters, revolutionized the industry. As his epitaph says, he "converted a rude and inconsiderable manufactory into an elegant art and an important part of the national commerce."

In this picture we are inside the Wedgwood factory, watching one of the most skillful operations in pottery making. This man is called a thrower. He throws a doughy-looking lump of clay on his potter's wheel, and then as the wheel revolves, his sensitive hands shape and mold the lump miraculously. Under the thrower's clay-covered fingers, the lump of clay seems to come to life. It rises from the spinning disk into the curving and graceful shape we see here, just as the potter intended.

Josiah Wedgwood was an exceptionally skilled thrower, as well as a scientist and businessman. Jasper ware, which we see in this picture, is the most famous of Josiah's creations, and it was his favorite. It is made in the well-known blue, green, yellow or black, and decorated with white classical reliefs like the vase in the background. Josiah Wedgwood was that rare genius who was able to unite art with industry.

At Stoke on the River Trent the Wedgwood pottery works turn out china that will be tomorrow's heirlooms.

69

NOTTINGHAM CASTLE: ROBIN HOOD'S COUNTRY

NOTTINGHAM is another thriving industrial city located almost in the center of England. But when we stand outside its castle walls high on a rocky hill, and see this bronze statue of Robin Hood, the centuries melt away and we are back in the Middle Ages. Howard Pyle's tales of the beloved outlaw caught the spirit of this scene in the opening lines:

> "In merry England in the time of old, when good King Henry the Second ruled the land, there lived within the green glades of Sherwood Forest, near Nottingham Town, a famous outlaw whose name was Robin Hood. No archer ever lived that could speed a gray goose shaft with such skill and cunning as his, nor were there ever such yeomen as the sevenscore merry men that roamed with him through the greenwood shades."

The greenwood shades are no more—much of the forest where the King's deer roamed has given way to ploughed fields, factories and coal mines. But the memory of Robin Hood is still alive. The tales of the outlawed nobleman who robbed the rich and defended the poor were handed down by word of mouth for centuries, and the story of Robin is part myth, part history. The poor and oppressed have always taken heart from these tales.

When Nottingham became a prosperous manufacturing city at the time of the industrial revolution, many of the old hand-weavers were thrown out of work by the new machines. The starving men rioted and smashed the hated mechanical looms. Much in the spirit of Robin Hood, a young lord who lived at Newstead Abbey just outside of Nottingham took up the cudgels for the rioters. Rising in the House of Lords to deliver his maiden speech, Lord Byron made an eloquent appeal for the dispossessed weavers. Robin Hood's horn seemed to sound again when the great poet spoke.

CHURCH AT HAWKSHEAD: THE LAKE DISTRICT

ENGLISH poets have found inspiration in many places—Kipling in India, Browning in Italy and blind Milton in an imaginary Paradise. But the lovely corner of England we are looking at here inspired its own group, the Lake poets, with its scenic grandeur. This little tract of land is only thirty-five miles square, yet it contains a remarkable diversity of scenes—lakes, mountains, valleys and old villages scarcely touched by the twentieth century.

We are standing above the churchyard in Hawkshead, a town near Lake Windermere, where the poet Wordsworth spent part of his childhood. He attended the sixteenth-century grammar school near the church, and one of the oak desks still has William's name carved on it. It was here among his native hills that Wordsworth was first stirred by the beauties of nature that he was to recollect so nobly in his later poetry. Not far from Hawkshead, beside a little lake, is the field where Wordsworth "wandered lonely as a cloud" and "saw a crowd, a host, of golden daffodils."

In the nineteenth century, the romantic landscapes of the Lake District attracted some of England's best-known writers. Coleridge, Shelley, Keats, Tennyson and Sir Walter Scott found this northern countryside conducive to creative work.

Today the Lake District is a National Park where Wordsworth's crowd of daffodils is almost outnumbered by throngs of vacationers. There is something for everyone here—boating, trout fishing, tennis, golf, woodland walks and mountain climbing. Though the highest mountain is only a little over 3,000 feet, rock climbing is challenging enough to interest Alpine experts, including one mountaineer who had tackled Everest. And for the non-athletes there is always a literary pilgrimage, combining the glories of English landscape and English literature in one fell swoop.

MUSEUM IN YORK: PERIOD ROOM

THE ancient city of York in the north of England is a museum in itself. The medieval ramparts that surround the town enclose treasures from England's varied past. In the magnificent cathedral of York Minster, a Saxon horn and a copy of the Saxon Gospels have been preserved. Roman ruins and a beautiful old Viking bowl are remnants of other conquerors. William, the greatest conqueror of them all, built two Norman castles here. The narrow, winding streets of York retain the atmosphere of the Middle Ages, and it is not surprising to come upon a little square called Whip ma Whop ma Gate, and be told that this is where disobedient wives used to be publicly whipped by their husbands. Other times, other customs.

York is fully aware of its rich past, and has sought to preserve it in intimate detail at one of the most fascinating places in the city. The

Museums in England preserve the splendid past, as in this portrait of Queen Elizabeth I.

Castle Museum of Yorkshire Bygones is as nostalgic as its name indicates. Here, in model rooms and streets, the life of northern England from 1500 to 1900 is affectionately recalled. As we stand on the threshold of this typical country room, we remember one of the best-loved stories of Yorkshire, *Lassie Come-Home*. And here, to the life, lies a collie like Lassie in just such a "small and humble" room as the one described in the story. Seeing it, those who have read the book feel that they too, have come home.

74

CAMBRIDGE UNIVERSITY: PUNTING ON THE CAM

THE ivy-covered walls of Cambridge remind Americans of their own universities, many of which have been built in this Gothic style. As a matter of fact, the link is stronger than mere architecture. John Harvard was a member of Emmanuel College in Cambridge, and he came to the Colonies and later founded the first university in America. The town where Harvard is located was named after Cambridge as a compliment to the founder's alma mater.

Three hundred years before America was discovered, scholars were gathering, first at Oxford, then at Cambridge, to study Latin, arithmetic, logic and astronomy. They sat on the floor in a room where a Master lectured or read from some rare and precious book while the students took notes in Latin. "Gentlemen" had no use for a university education in the Middle Ages. But the clever sons of lower-middle-class families were the tattered scholars who hoped to better their stations in life.

Poor boys were sent to get their education at the age of fourteen, and it soon became apparent that they needed supervision, decent places where they could eat and sleep, and financial help. That was why the colleges were founded. Both Oxford and Cambridge have their fair share of illustrious alumni—but Cambridge, with Newton and Darwin and some of the present-day atomic physicists, seems to have a slight edge in the sciences.

In this picture of a lazy undergraduate afternoon, we are looking at St. John's College with its "Bridge of Sighs" spanning the Cam. Within the mellow buildings, the intellectual riches of an entire civilization are waiting to be unlocked. But youth is a time for dreaming, too, and generations of earnest scholars have set aside their books for an afternoon of punting on the Cam.

CEREMONY IN LONDON: AGE-OLD POMP

AGAINST the new green of a London spring, the immemorial pageantry of the Crown is seen once more. When the great royal coaches roll down the Mall, they seem to be a part of a longer parade that stretches far back into England's past. From rough Saxon chieftain to modern monarch, the line of English rulers spans the splendid centuries.

As we join the people watching this stately ceremonial, we realize that the white horses, the scarlet and black and gold uniforms, and the gilded coaches are more than mere trappings of good showmanship. They stand for the Crown, and the Crown encompasses all of English history. The future is here, too, glimpsed through the window of a passing coach where a small prince waves to the crowds he will one day rule.

This city that has lived through fire and plague and air-raid bombardments is smiling and fair once again on a May morning. Its citizens are free men and women with a great heritage of literature, art and the noblest institutions of democracy. Their valiant English spirit will live through the years in Churchill's ringing words:

"The Mother of Parliaments" rises from the bank of the Thames, a noble symbol of the rights of free men.

"We shall defend our island, whatever the cost may be, we shall fight on the beaches, we shall fight on the landing grounds, we shall fight in the fields and in the streets, we shall fight in the hills; we shall never surrender."

SOME IMPORTANT DATES IN ENGLISH HISTORY

1200 B.C.-600 B.C.	*Prehistoric inhabitants of Britain are the Celts. Priestly Druids preside over religion.*
57 B.C.-450 A.D.	*Roman occupation of Britain begins with conquest by Julius Caesar. Later expeditions under Roman emperors Claudius and Hadrian complete the transformation of Celtic Britain into a Roman province. With the decline of Rome, the island returns to a low state of civilization.*
450-800	*Influx of Germanic tribes leads to establishment of several Anglo-Saxon kingdoms, united in 825 under Egbert of Wessex.*
871-899	*Alfred the Great defeats Danish invaders. England is divided— the south under Alfred's rule, the northeast under Danes. Alfred is first great patron of learning.*
1017-1035	*After continued Viking invasions, Canute becomes ruler of Denmark, Norway and England.*
1066	*Battle of Hastings; William the Conqueror invades England from Normandy and seizes throne.*
1154	*Henry II, first Plantagenet king, ascends the throne.*
1215	*King John signs Magna Charta at Runnymede. Basic human rights, including trial by jury, are thenceforth assured by law.*
1337	*Beginning of Hundred Years' War. Forces of France and England are engaged in battles of Crécy, Poitiers, Agincourt and Orléans.*
1431	*Joan of Arc is burned by the British at Rouen.*
1455-1485	*The Wars of the Roses, between houses of Lancaster and York for the Crown of England, end when Henry VII becomes first Tudor king.*
1534	*Henry VIII establishes the Church of England after breaking with Rome.*
1558-1603	*Reign of Elizabeth I is England's golden age of literature, exploration and national strength.*
1588	*Defeat of the "invincible" Spanish Armada secures England's supremacy of the seas.*
1603	*James I becomes first Stuart king.*
1607	*First permanent English settlement in North America is established at Jamestown, Virginia.*
1649	*King Charles I is beheaded during Civil War.*
1649-1660	*Oliver Cromwell is Lord Protector of the Commonwealth of England, Scotland and Ireland.*
1660	*The monarchy is restored under Charles II.*
1707	*England and Scotland unite to become Great Britain.*
1714	*George I becomes first Hanoverian king. (House of Hanover is renamed House of Windsor in 1917.)*
1775-1783	*War of American Independence begins at Concord bridge, Massachusetts, and ends with Treaty of Paris.*
1801	*Great Britain and Ireland unite under name of United Kingdom.*
1815	*Battle of Waterloo ends Napoleonic Wars.*
1837-1901	*Reign of Victoria.*
1914-1918	*World War I; Treaty of Versailles is signed June 28, 1919.*
1939-1945	*World War II; after the end of the war, the United Kingdom becomes one of the original members of the United Nations.*
1952	*Elizabeth II becomes Queen of England.*

SOME FAMOUS NAMES IN ENGLISH HISTORY

ALFRED THE GREAT (849-899)—*Most successful monarch of Saxon line and major figure in England's development; saved England from the Danes.*

WILLIAM THE CONQUEROR (1027-1087)—*Norman duke who defeated King Harold at Hastings to gain the English throne.*

THOMAS À BECKET (1118?-1170)—*Archbishop of Canterbury who tried to restrict royal power and was murdered in Canterbury Cathedral by overzealous knights of Henry II; later canonized.*

SIR THOMAS MORE (1478-1535)—*Reformer and author of* Utopia, *executed by Henry VIII for refusing to recognize king's authority over church; canonized 1935.*

ELIZABETH I (1533-1603)—*Daughter of Henry VIII and Anne Boleyn; courageously guided England through a period of political and religious strife.*

SIR FRANCIS DRAKE (1540?-1596)—*Privateer, Royal Admiral who defeated Spanish Armada and helped to establish England as mistress of the seas.*

WILLIAM SHAKESPEARE (1564-1616)—*"The Bard of Avon." One of the world's greatest dramatists and poets.*

OLIVER CROMWELL (1599-1658)—*Puritan and military leader; overthrew Charles I and established the Puritan Commonwealth and Protectorate (1653-58).*

SIR CHRISTOPHER WREN (1632-1723)—*Famous architect whose best-known work is St. Paul's Cathedral in London.*

SAMUEL JOHNSON (1709-1784)—*Lexicographer, author and wit.*

JAMES BOSWELL (1740-1795)—*Brilliant biographer of Dr. Johnson.*

THOMAS GAINSBOROUGH (1727-1788)—*Artist famous for portraiture; his* Blue Boy *is a perennial favorite.*

EDWARD GIBBON (1737-1794)—*Famed historian best known for his definitive work,* The History of the Decline and Fall of the Roman Empire.

LORD HORATIO NELSON (1758-1805)—*Great naval hero, killed just at the moment of victory in the Battle of Trafalgar against the French.*

PERCY BYSSHE SHELLEY (1792-1822)—*Poet, best known for romantic "Ode to a Nightingale." His wife Mary was the author of* Frankenstein.

GEORGE GORDON, LORD BYRON (1788-1824)—*Romantic poet who wrote "Prisoner of Chillon" and "Childe Harold's Pilgrimage."*

JOHN STUART MILL (1806-1873)—*Philosopher, author of "Essay on Liberty."*

CHARLES DARWIN (1809-1882)—*Author of theory of evolution in* The Origin of Species, *most important work of modern biology (1859).*

BENJAMIN DISRAELI (1804-1881)—*Politician, author and Prime Minister under Victoria; responsible for British participation in the Suez Canal.*

QUEEN VICTORIA (1819-1901)—*Her sixty-four-year reign was the longest of any British sovereign, a period of tremendous social reform and growth.*

WINSTON CHURCHILL (1874-1965)—*Great statesman, author and Prime Minister (1940-1945 and 1951-1955); England's mainstay during World War II.*

SOME DIFFERENCES IN ENGLISH AND AMERICAN USAGE

Although the Englishman and the American share a common language, there are some words that are peculiar to each country. Here is a list of some English words translated into American-English.

ENGLISH	AMERICAN	ENGLISH	AMERICAN
bobby	policeman	pram	baby carriage
char	cleaning woman	goods train	freight train
clerk (clark)	clerical help (not salesperson)	hoarding	billboard
		lift	elevator
dustman	garbage man	lorry	truck
ironmonger	hardware dealer	mudguard	fender
to black	to shine shoes (any color)	omnibus	bus
		tram	streetcar or trolley
boots	shoes	tube	subway
braces	suspenders	petrol	gasoline
suspenders	garters	return	round-trip ticket
vest	undershirt	roundabout	merry-go-round
waistcoat	vest	spanner	monkey-wrench
flannel	washcloth	minerals	soda water or soft drinks
flat	apartment		
garden	backyard	sweets	dessert
geyser	water heater	savoury	spicy course after dessert
toll call	local call		
trunk call	long distance call	serviette	napkin
bank holiday	any holiday	leader	editorial
cheerio	goodbye	fortnight	two weeks

Although the value of foreign currency fluctuates from time to time, the following rate of exchange for English currency has been stable for several years.

ENGLISH MONEY	VALUE	WRITTEN
pound, or quid	$2.80	£1
half-crown	35¢	2/6
shilling, or bob	14¢	1/
sixpence, or tanner	7¢	6d.
threepence (THRUP-*pence*)	3½¢	3d.
penny	1¢	1d.
half penny (HAYP-*nee*)	½¢	½d.

INDEX